D0450509

THE PARENT'S GUIDE TO
TEACHING SELF-DEFENSE

THE PARENT'S GUIDE TO
TEACHING SELF-DEFENSE

Paul McCallum

BETTERWAY BOOKS

CINCINNATI, OHIO

The Parent's Guide to Teaching Self-Defense. Copyright © 1994 by Paul Mc-Callum. Printed and bound in the United States of America. All rights reserved. No part of this book may be reproduced in any form or by any electronic or mechanical means including information storage and retrieval systems without permission in writing from the publisher, except by a reviewer, who may quote brief passages in a review. Published by Betterway Books, an imprint of F&W Publications, Inc., 1507 Dana Avenue, Cincinnati, Ohio 45207. 1-800-289-0963. First edition.

98   97   96   95   94   5   4   3   2   1

Library of Congress Cataloging-in-Publication Data

McCallum, Paul
      The parent's guide to teaching self-defense / by Paul McCallum.
          p.   cm.
      Includes index.
      ISBN 1-55870-346-2
      1. Self-defense for children. I. Title.
GV1111.4.M37   1994
                                                                    94-1049
                                                                    CIP

Edited by Mary Sproles
Designed by Sandy Conopeotis
Front cover photos by D. Altman Fleischer

Betterway Books are available at special discounts for sales promotions, premiums and fund-raising use. Special editions or book excerpts can also be created to specification. For details contact: Special Sales Director, Betterway Books, 1507 Dana Avenue, Cincinnati, Ohio 45207.

613.66
MCC
1994

This book is dedicated to
Zuleika

ABOUT THE AUTHOR

Paul McCallum was ten when he developed an interest in self-defense. Since then he has studied and taught several martial arts styles. He is the author of *A Practical Self-Defense Guide for Women*.

Paul is also a diving instructor, photographer and the author of seven books. He has also written many magazine articles and his photography has appeared in several publications. His specialty is sports and the outdoors.

Paul lives in Los Angeles with his wife Christine.

ACKNOWLEDGMENTS

Barry Krause—for helping me carry equipment around during the photo shoots and for editing the original manuscript.

A special note of gratitude to Maria Doest and the young students at Karate Women, who posed for the numerous photos in this book. Their help was invaluable.

Mary Sproles—for her excellent editing and patience.

All the martial arts instructors I've trained with over the years, particularly Dave Scully and Hawkins Cheung.

Bob Hostage and the staff at Betterway Books—it's been a fun run!

DISCLAIMER

The publisher and the author do not assume any responsibility for how the information presented in this book is interpreted or used. The nature of self-defense training makes injuries possible, so extreme caution should be exercised at all times when practicing with a partner. Readers are solely responsible for any liability that may occur as a result of their actions.

INTRODUCTION   1
Are You Qualified to Teach? • Self-Defense vs. Sport
Defense • Age to Start • Be Realistic • Clothing

Chapter One   **TEACHING SELF-DEFENSE**   6
Keep It Simple • Philosophy • Emotional Sensitivity •
Teach Responsibility

Chapter Two   **PRACTICE SESSIONS**   12
Sparring With a Partner • Practice With Equipment •
Practice Alone • Practice Often • Length of Practice

Chapter Three **THE BASIC FIGHTING STANCE**   20

Chapter Four   **KICKS**   23
Sequence of Instruction • Round Kick • Front Kick • Side
Kick • Stepping Side Kick • Spin Kick • Foot Stomp

Chapter Five   **HITTING WITH THE HANDS**   43
Front Punch • Reverse Punch • Palm Strike • Karate
Chop • Ridge Hand

Chapter Six   **BLOCKING**   53
Teaching Kids How to Block • Overhead Block • Inside
Block • Downward Block • Downward Cross Block •
Outside Block

Chapter Seven **ESCAPING CHOKES AND HOLDS**   66
Rear Choke Hold • Bear Hug • Single Wrist Grabs •
Single Wrist Grab #1 • Single Wrist Grab #2 • Single
Wrist Grab #3 • Single Wrist Grab #4 • Single Wrist
Grab #5 • Single Wrist Grab #6 • Grabbed by Both
Wrists • Grabbed by the Hair • Front Choke • Rear
Choke • Shoulder Grab • Grabbed on Both Sides

Chapter Eight **IN THE STREET** **91**
Picked Up Off the Ground • Against a Wall • Pushed •
Hair Grab • Attempted Shoulder Grab • Shoulder Grab
• Slapped • Pushed to the Ground • Head Lock • Pushed
Into a Corner • Against a Gang • Harassed • Front Grab

Chapter Nine **PSYCHOLOGY AND TACTICS** **117**
Think Self-Defense • First Strike • Screaming • Choices
• Avoiding Trouble • Misdirection • Gender Differences

Chapter Ten **STYLES AND SCHOOLS** **123**
Styles • Schools • Conclusion

INDEX **129**

INTRODUCTION

This book deals with self-defense. I define self-defense as the ability to repel and disable an attacker within a few seconds. This book is about teaching your children how to get away from an assailant—and how to do it fast. Self-defense may involve a single block followed by two quick punches and a kick. The idea is that your children can run away after they have momentarily stunned or injured their opponent. This concept of self-defense is different than the concept of knowing how to fight. This book isn't about how to prepare your children for a fight that may last several minutes. The longer a fight lasts, the lower the chances of a successful escape.

ARE YOU QUALIFIED TO TEACH?

Before you jump in and begin showing techniques to your children, you must ask yourself if you are qualified to teach your children self-defense. Do you have any martial arts experience? If you don't, you will still be able to teach your child some self-defense from the information presented in this book. However, I wouldn't recommend it as your only resource. It takes a long time to master the basics of self-defense, and it takes years to learn self-defense well enough to teach it to someone else. You would be doing your children an injustice if you were to teach them something incorrectly, especially since this misinformation could result in injuries.

Self-defense training will give your child the ability to handle situations such as this!

I'm not saying you need to be a black belt or professional boxer to be qualified to teach your kids, but I do feel that you should have some previous experience with the basics.

That said, I do feel that any exposure to self-defense is better than no exposure. It's really a personal judgment as to whether or not you are qualified to teach your children how to defend themselves. Did you know that many self-defense classes for children cost as little as thirty dollars a month? One option is to enroll your children in a class in addition to coaching them outside of class. This book can also be used to educate yourself about some of the things they will be learning in their class.

SELF-DEFENSE VS. SPORT DEFENSE

This book focuses on practical self-defense. The methods taught here are intended for use by children when confronted with a potentially dangerous situation. Generally, you will begin teaching street self-defense. Your children should be taught to defend themselves against aggressors. Low kicks, simple punches, escapes from different types of holds, and an understanding of some of the tactics involved when defending oneself are basics of this teaching.

There are some overlaps between sport and self-defense techniques, but there are different techniques designed for sport than those aimed towards disabling a mugger. For example, a side kick to the knee can break someone's leg—definitely a street defense tactic. A side kick delivered to the stomach will result in less damage, which could be used in the street *or* in a tournament. A side kick to the head, although damaging if delivered with enough force, is difficult to execute and therefore is primarily a sport technique.

While I believe in teaching sport self-defense as well as street self-defense, it is important to make it clear to your students that there is a difference between the two. Some techniques, such as high kicks to the head are difficult to perform and generally require a warm-up. Obviously, most attackers don't allow their victims the luxury of going through a warm-up routine. A front kick, on the other hand, can be executed easily and without a warm-up in almost any situation.

So what techniques should you teach? This book contains simple, effective, self-defense techniques that have been proven to be effective by my own experiences and those of some of my students. There are also a few examples of what I consider to be sport techniques. These are included because they are fun to learn and because they help develop coordination. Basically, when you teach a move, ask yourself if you think it would be effective if it had to be used to fend off an attack.

AGE TO START

One question many parents ask is, "How old should my children be before they can begin self-defense training?" I recommend training only children who are four years old or older. Even then, "training" is a relative word.

Introducing four-year-olds to martial arts should be conducted as a play session, not serious self-defense training. Hold soft bags for them to hit and don't let them strike with any force. Under no circumstances should you attempt to introduce them to the concept of hitting another child. Your only goal is to expose them to the type of coordination involved in kicking and punching.

Hitting bags is a lot of fun for children and they seem to really enjoy it. I have found that it's a good idea also to introduce some simple tumbling exercises when teaching young children. Try to use a wide variety of activities to keep the children entertained and to hold their interest long enough to teach them some basics.

Give girls the opportunity to practice on boys who are larger and stronger.

Once a child is about five or six years old, you can begin to conduct more formalized training sessions. By formalized, I mean you can teach classes that have a structure and routine. Most children younger than five simply become bored in these types of classes.

You will be the best judge of what type of class will best suit your child. I have seen some four-year-olds participate in formalized karate training—often in adult classes. I've also seen some seven-year-old kids who didn't have the discipline to stay with a one-hour class.

Six-year-olds to teenagers can definitely be taught self-defense in an organized class. Don't worry about mixing age groups—it's beneficial and gives young children the chance to practice against older kids. Same

Even young children can learn how to deal with these types of problems through self-defense training.

thing for mixing the sexes. Chances are, if your daughter ever needs to defend herself, she will most likely have to defend herself against a male. Practicing her punches and kicks against boys will help give her the needed confidence.

BE REALISTIC

It's critical to your child's safety that you don't instill false confidence. For example, it's unrealistic to think that an eight-year-old child is going to develop the ability to fend off an assault from a two-hundred-pound adult male. Make sure your child has a realistic view of his self-defense capabilities.

It's easy for children to make the mistake of equating martial arts ability with superhuman strength. Movies and television expose youngsters to heroes who have the ability to conquer dozens of individuals with kung fu. Naturally, your students may assume that their newfound knowledge will give them such powers. While it is important for them to experience success, it is also important that they realize their limitations. They should not *always* win, because this will create false confidence. Pitting children against others of differing size and ability will give them a "reality check." Six-year-olds need to realize that they cannot take on an adult (although we will discuss ways they can escape an attack by an adult). Always emphasize the importance of defending *in order to get away*, not to be superkid.

CLOTHING

It's not necessary to buy your child a karate gi (outfit). Sweat pants, gym shorts, running shorts, or any type of loose clothing is adequate for training at home.

Have the kids work out in bare feet. Naturally, you should conduct your classes in an area that is conducive to being shoeless. One of the best solutions is to buy a few large padded mats that can be rolled up when not in use. This way you'll have the option of teaching indoors or outdoors.

It's a good idea to have your students work out occasionally while wearing "street clothes." The odds of a child being attacked while wearing workout clothes is relatively slim! Tight jeans, for example, will restrict freedom of movement and make kicking difficult. Heavy winter coats can also restrict movement. Does your child wear padded gloves when it's cold? These may make punches relatively ineffective. Wearing street clothes will enable you and your students to discover any restrictions imposed by the clothes.

Chapter One

TEACHING SELF-DEFENSE

Now that we've looked at what to wear and when to start, let's look at how to begin.

KEEP IT SIMPLE

One of the most important concepts in teaching self-defense techniques is: keep things simple. If your children have to defend themselves against a school-yard bully, a mugger on the street or a pervert, chances are they will be scared. Trying to execute a complicated series of self-defense maneuvers that require above-average coordination will be difficult at best. To increase your children's chances of success, stick to simple techniques that are easy to execute under the stress of an attack. For example, jumping in the air to execute a spinning back kick may look terrific in the gym, but could have serious consequences if it doesn't work in the street. A front kick, on the other hand, is easy to remember and simple to perform.

I've always taught my students that simplicity is the key to success. If a bully is picking on your child, a simple punch to the nose followed up by a front kick to the stomach will probably be an extremely effective deterrent to the aggressor. Conversely, attempting to execute a bewildering combination of spinning kicks and complicated hand techniques may result in failure.

As mentioned earlier, children need to experience success if they are to have the confidence to defend themselves. If you teach your children complicated techniques that fail to work when needed, this may seriously damage their confidence in future encounters. I realize not all fights are won, but don't stack the odds against your children by teaching a system that doesn't work.

PHILOSOPHY

Teaching children requires a different approach than teaching adults. One of the keys to success with children is to structure the class in a way that is fun and entertaining. Here are some concepts you should keep in mind when teaching children.

Teach One Thing at a Time

It's better to focus on one skill at a time than to attempt to introduce multiple skills simultaneously. Most students end up retaining very little of what they are taught if you bombard them with too much information. The best way to conduct your classes is to introduce one skill at a time, and then practice that skill slowly and without power. After the basic coordination for the move has been developed, you can begin to let them hit the bag with a little force.

The next step is to introduce a second skill in the same manner. For most beginners, four skills is about the maximum that should be introduced per class. If you combine two or more of these skills, the students actually get exposed to a tremendous amount of information. However, don't start putting combinations together until the kids have mastered the individual kicks and punches.

Most people find that their bodies and brains become comfortable with certain techniques, and children aren't any different. Encourage your children to develop speed and power with the techniques they find comfortable. For example, it's much more beneficial to be able to deliver a front kick with crippling force than to be able to execute five different kicks ineffectively. You will probably find that each student's "internal memory" will retain certain moves. Help them develop the techniques they like (but don't ignore trouble areas).

Pay Attention to Each Child

Learning self-defense can be very intimidating to some children, especially if they are in class with older or bigger kids. It is easy to accidentally overlook a particular individual when you are teaching a large group. Ironically, the quietest child in your class may be the one who is in need of the most attention. Make a point of always working with each of your students individually during each class.

Keep Classes Fun

If your training sessions aren't enjoyable, your students will lose interest. Try creating some games to keep the classes from becom-

Learning self-defense can be a lot of fun for kids.

ing too routine. For example, bring a large hoop to one of your classes and have the kids jump through it and land on their feet, or have them dive through it and execute a shoulder roll back into a standing position (use a padded mat). Another possibility is to lay a large bag on the ground and have the kids jump over it and execute a flying side kick into a hand-held bag.

Keep in mind that games of this nature are used to develop coordination while enabling the kids to have fun. Don't view children's self-defense with the same practicality you would adult self-defense. It's okay for the kids to have fun practicing things that an adult might find impractical in a self-defense situation. The more comfortable children become with the moves, the more likely they are to be able to execute them effectively if necessary.

Keep Them Moving

A sure way to lose a student's interest is to spend a lot of time standing around talking. Practicing self-defense is a lot of fun for most children and they will probably be anxious to start kicking and punching. While adults and teenagers may benefit from verbal descriptions, a lecture will usually put children to sleep — at which point they start kicking and punching each other anyway. Don't waste time standing around talking.

Compliment Good Performance

I know this sounds obvious, but it's easy to forget. Make a point of acknowledging the fact that a child has done something well. Children generally want to please adults and feel a sense of pride when their accomplishments are acknowledged, especially if a parent is involved. Your children will probably work harder if they feel you are proud of their progress.

Don't Compare the Children

Adults can deal with being compared to other students for the sake of making a point; children usually can't. If a student is having trouble mastering a particular move, the last thing he wants to be told is to watch his younger sibling who is doing it right. Use yourself as an example rather than another child.

Watch Your Strength

It's easy to forget your own strength when teaching martial arts. While you may have no difficulty controlling your kicks and punches with young kids, it's easy to accidentally bring things up to speed with teenagers who may weigh as much as you.

EMOTIONAL SENSITIVITY

Always remember that you are the adult and that you are dealing with children. There is a psychological factor to be considered when a father spars with his son. It would be unfair of you to push your teenage son across an emotional threshold he may not be prepared for. For example, he may not want to hit you as hard as he would a peer. In addition, it may be upsetting if you begin to "wale" on your child under the umbrella of self-defense instruction.

Obviously, daughters should clearly be given the same consideration, particularly in mother/daughter situations. Also, keep in mind that young girls are developing physically and may be self-conscious about being grabbed by boys in the class. While a thirteen-year-old boy may have no trouble with another boy grabbing him in a bear hug, a young girl might be a little more self-conscious. You probably

Always supervise any physical contact to prevent injuries. Stress safety and responsibility.

are sensitive to your own child's psychology. However, it's easy to overlook it in other kids you may teach or to forget the needs of younger children if your kids are well beyond a certain stage of development.

TEACH RESPONSIBILITY

It is important that children understand the morality involved with inflicting painful injury upon another person. They must be made aware of what self-defense techniques can do to another person. Much of the responsibility must be assumed by you; don't teach lethal techniques to young children. Clearly, you don't want your seven-year-old daughter to chop another little girl in the throat and break her wind pipe because she took her doll during recess. Once again, *don't teach lethal techniques to children who don't have the maturity to know when not to use them.*

Educate the kids about the consequences of hurting another person. Your students may not have any previous exposure to violent encounters — they don't know what kicking somebody in the ribs will do to them. For example, I recently taught a seminar to a group

of seventh-graders at a local school. After discussing front kicks—
which the class had been slowly practicing without power for about
ten minutes—I asked for a volunteer to come up so I could demonstrate how the technique would be used against an adult male. A
young girl joined me in front of the class and, before I could say a
word, hauled off and kicked me as hard as she could in the groin.
Fortunately, I was wearing a cup!

The student's kick wasn't an act of aggression—she simply didn't
know what the consequences were of kicking a man in the groin.
It was a valuable lesson to me, as it demonstrated how unaware
kids can be about the consequences of hitting somebody. Explain
to your students exactly what each blow will do. If you don't, you
may be in for a nasty surprise and a possible lawsuit if your child
seriously injures another person without just cause.

Keep in mind that most adults aren't prepared to be attacked by
children, and your children probably don't believe they are capable
of injuring an adult. You don't want your students to attack an adult
"for fun" because they don't think they will injure the grown-up.
The girl who kicked me during the class simply took it for granted
that she was incapable of hurting a martial arts instructor.

Chapter Two

PRACTICE SESSIONS

Children can practice their self-defense techniques with a partner (sparring), against equipment and alone.

Before allowing children to engage in any form of contact sparring, you should purchase adequate safety equipment to cut down on the risk of injury. I recommend gloves, foot pads, head gear, chest protectors, groin cups, shin pads, and mouth pieces all be used. There's absolutely no reason to risk injuries to your children because they weren't wearing the proper safety equipment.

You can wear protective equipment and let your kids practice their techniques at full speed and power. This is a great way for them to train.

SPARRING WITH A PARTNER

The best way to develop your children's ability is to have them practice with a partner. One way to practice with a partner is to use training equipment that the kids take turns holding. Another way is to let them actually spar against each other. One advantage of teaching your children yourself is that you can probably let them hit you with greater force than they could another child. Presumably, you can absorb a young child's round kick to your arms without sustaining any damage.

Kids should be allowed to practice on adults to build confidence and ability.

One-Step Sparring

One-step sparring involves practicing a prearranged series of moves against an opponent. For example, one child throws a punch to the head, and the other child executes a block followed up by a reverse punch to the ribs. Do not allow kids to make hard contact. They can speed things up once they have worked out the coordination, but don't let them actually hit each other with any force.

"One-step" sparring can actually involve many "steps." It's the concept of practicing prearranged moves that you want to keep in mind. The benefit of this type of practice is that students begin to get an understanding of how to combine the assorted kicks, punches, and blocks they've learned into a flowing sequence. I understand that it's generally not possible to execute a prearranged sequence of moves in a street fight. But that's not really what the goal is with one-step sparring. The goal is to introduce your child to the coordination and timing involved in a physical confrontation with another person.

One-Step Contact

This is one-step sparring with a little contact. The idea is that students are allowed to hit each other *lightly* at midspeed and later at full speed, but are still executing a prearranged sequence of moves.

The goal of this type of training is to introduce students to the feel of moving with more speed, while still retaining the safety of a prearranged routine. Allowing the kids to hit each other lightly in safe areas such as the stomach, arms, and legs also introduces them to the feel of contact. It's important that your children get over any fears they have of being hit if they are to defend themselves successfully in a fight. Naturally, you must closely supervise how much contact is allowed.

Speed is an important factor when executing self-defense techniques. Encourage your children to develop their speed with one-step sparring.

No-Contact Free Sparring

After your children have some experience with one-step sparring, introduce them to free sparring. Free sparring is basically a controlled fight. Two opponents square off and fight each other *with control.* The opponents can be two children, you and your child, children of the opposite sex, or children of different age groups. In fact, exposing your child to different types of opponents can be a good way to build confidence and reinforce reality.

At this stage of the game, don't allow the kids to hit each other at all (except to block their opponent's kicks and punches). Why? Because they don't yet have the necessary skill to avoid injury. The goal with no-contact sparring is to develop a feel for the distance and timing involved in a fight. I realize that this type of sparring isn't that realistic, but it's as close as you can get in training without risking undue injury to your students.

Initially, instruct your students to move slowly, without speed or power. There's no point to letting them smash up their arms and legs at this stage. Encourage them to experiment with the different moves they have learned. If something doesn't work, analyze what they are doing wrong and strive to correct the problem.

An additional benefit to free sparring without contact is it will introduce shy children to free sparring without risk of injury. It's critical that children overcome their fear of physical contact if they are to defend themselves during an attack. No-contact free sparring allows kids to get used to seeing punches and kicks coming at them without having to experience being hit. This is the first step toward becoming comfortable with the concept of free sparring.

Light-Contact Free Sparring

Light-contact free sparring allows the opponents to hit each other with light to moderate force. *It is imperative that you monitor sparring activities closely since it's easy for sparring to escalate into a full-contact fight without supervision.*

Protective gear such as this can be bought at most martial arts stores or through the mail order sections of many martial arts magazines.

The goal is to give the children a realistic feel for what it's like to be in a fight. Obviously, sparring of this nature should only be conducted after months of basic training.

Keep in mind that this is *light* contact. The safety equipment is worn primarily as a precautionary measure. While light head contact can be allowed, don't let the kids hit each other in the head with any substantial force. Also, blows to the knees, elbows, neck, groin, and other sensitive areas should be avoided—even with safety equipment.

You can also reintroduce prearranged sparring techniques at this stage. The idea is to teach your students exactly how much contact is allowed before giving them the freedom to hit at will.

One of the primary purposes of light-contact free sparring is to get your students used to being hit. This can't be overemphasized. I'm not suggesting that your children need to be comfortable when somebody hits them hard, but they need to accept the fact that they may be hit during an encounter and that not all blows result in damage.

Full-Contact Sparring

Full-contact sparring should only be conducted by experts who have the skill to handle these types of conditions. While some older teenagers may have the skill to handle full-contact sparring while wearing full body armor, young kids shouldn't be allowed to engage in full contact under any circumstances.

Full-contact sparring is simply an all-out fight between two opponents; obviously full body protection must be worn. About the only things that aren't allowed in full contact are crippling techniques such as kicks to the knee, eye jabs, and strikes to the throat. Full-contact sparring is used primarily in sports competition and should not be attempted by amateur instructors or students.

PRACTICE WITH EQUIPMENT

Another way for your child to work out is to practice against equipment. This can be done alone or with a partner. Before you begin teaching your child self-defense, I highly recommend you visit a martial arts supply store. Depending on your budget, you may opt to buy only a few hand-held bags, or go for a more complete setup with a heavy bag, weights, humanoid dummies, and other equipment to suit your particular needs. Keep in mind, however, that it is possible to teach self-defense with very little equipment.

One of the best ways to practice and learn self-defense techniques is to kick or punch a bag that is held by a partner. Practicing in this manner will help give children a realistic "feel" for the distances involved when hitting another individual. It also allows them to get an idea of how hard they have to kick to move someone.

Start these practice sessions at slow speed until the students have a good understanding of the coordination involved. In the beginning, their training partner should stand still while holding the bag to provide a solid target. Once the students have an understanding

You may want to invest in a heavy bag. It is great for practicing safely with power.

of the move, they can begin to incorporate more speed and power.

You can make the training even more realistic by allowing your students to move around each other while kicking or punching the bag (after they have developed some ability). Explain that it's unlikely that an attacker will simply stand still and allow himself to be kicked and punched. When the partner who is holding the bag has the freedom to move around, it forces the child kicking to work out the distances and timing required to hit a moving opponent. It's an extremely realistic way of training. Remember to have the kids alternate holding the bag and striking the bag. For example, have them switch after every ten kicks or punches.

There are a seemingly endless variety of bags designed to be held by training partners. In addition to the large bags, there are also a lot of "focus gloves" that are worn on the hand to create a fast-moving live target. To keep things interesting for your kids, you may want to invest in a diverse selection of equipment.

You can also purchase equipment that your child can practice on when alone. A heavy bag hung from a tree or beam in your house is excellent. However, before you hang any bags in your house or garage (or any structure), make sure the building can support the weight of the bag and the stress that will be created when people kick and punch it. Another option is to buy one of the heavy bags that are designed to stand on the floor unassisted. In addition, there are also a few free-standing holding stands available if you don't want to hang a bag up.

It's important to remember that children's bones are still growing. Don't let children engage in any of the "bone toughening" exercises that are used by some martial artists. Avoid anything that could damage young bones, such as punching beanbags permanently attached to walls as used in some martial art styles. Stick to punching bags that have some give for all-out punching.

If you have a solid wall or post, you may want to attach a small pad that children can punch *lightly*. Don't allow them to hit full power since this may result in bone damage. The idea is to let them hit something solid in addition to "punching the air."

PRACTICE ALONE

Your child can practice alone if a training partner isn't available. Actually, this a very traditional way to train in some martial arts. Many styles teach students "katas" (also called forms) which are basically a series of moves that are memorized, and then performed in sequence. Katas are a major part of the learning process in most kung fu and karate systems.

I'm not suggesting you teach your children katas, but I do suggest that you encourage them to practice their kicks and punches by themselves. Instruct them to go through the moves slowly, without speed or power. You want them to gain an understanding of the coordination involved with each move before they begin to hit with any speed or power. Your children can also practice their moves toward a stationary object, such as a wall or tree. Tell them to stop a few inches away and not to make contact with the target. The idea is to begin to learn about the distances involved. All practicing at this stage should be done slowly and without power.

PRACTICE OFTEN

It is important that your children practice often. How often? Practicing self-defense three times a week is ideal. I've found that beginning students don't retain information if they practice less fre-

ALBUQUERQUE ACADEMY
LIBRARY

When a partner is unavailable, techniques can be practiced alone.

quently. Conversely, you don't want the kids to burn out.

Keep in mind that you don't necessarily have to supervise all the practice sessions. After a skill has been introduced and practiced under your supervision, children can rehearse movements on their own. As mentioned above, children can practice on their own with or without equipment.

LENGTH OF PRACTICE

How long should your training sessions be? Young kids often have fairly short attention spans, while older children may be able to stay focused through a two-hour class. As a guideline, keep classes roughly half an hour in length for children under six years old, one to two hours for six- to eleven-year-olds, and two hours or longer for preteens and teenagers. These are rough guidelines that should be adjusted to suit children's attention spans.

Chapter Three

THE BASIC FIGHTING STANCE

The first thing you should teach children is the basic fighting stance. The easiest way is to simply copy the form in the following photographs. Explain that presenting a profile provides their opponent with a smaller target area. A good example is to show them how much harder it is to kick or hit them in the groin when they're standing backwards.

Show your children how they should hold their hands. Explain that the front hand guards the upper body and the rear hand guards the lower body. Of course, there will be times when these roles reverse.

Explain that the feet should be about shoulder-width apart with the rear leg slightly bent.

The basic fighting stance as viewed from the front.

The basic fighting stance as viewed from the side.

When you teach the kids how to kick, point out that they should always hold their hands in the basic ready position.

Note how the girl kicking hasn't dropped her guard.

Explain how the front hand can be dropped to block a kick if necessary.

Chapter Four

KICKS

Kicks have many advantages in a self-defense situation—two of the biggest are power and distance.

Most people's legs are a lot stronger than their arms. While children may not have enough upper-body strength to hit a bigger child with damaging power, they probably do possess more than adequate leg strength. A small girl, for example, can drop a larger boy with a well-placed kick to the groin.

Kicks also give your children the advantage of distance. When their kick lands, they will be out of range of the aggressor's fists. There are obvious advantages to staying out of range of an opponent's hands. Kicking also lets your children begin their defense from a few feet away.

Incidentally, kicking an opponent doesn't require that the student start a few feet away. It's possible—and effective—to deliver devastating kicks while standing right next to an attacker. Knowing how to kick will give children the option to choose which tactic is best for whatever situation they may encounter.

Most of the kicks that follow are demonstrated with the rear foot for two reasons. The first is the distance factor; the second is power. Kicking with the rear leg builds up more momentum than kicking with the front leg. However, have the kids practice all the kicks with both their front and rear legs.

SEQUENCE OF INSTRUCTION

The method of teaching discussed here should be applied to all the techniques in this book. Although a round kick (a.k.a. "round house") is demonstrated in the following pictures, you should follow the same sequence of instruction regardless of whether you're teaching a kick, punch or release. Begin with guided practice, slowly walking the children through the motions, then supervise their practicing alone until they are comfortable with all movements involved. Only then should a target be introduced.

Always do some light stretches with your kids before working out.

It is particularly important to warm up the legs before practicing kicks.

ROUND KICK

The round kick has many applications and can be an extremely powerful weapon. Low round kicks can be used as a sweep or a painful strike to the upper thigh; round kicks to the groin, ribs and stomach are ideal for school-yard defense; and practicing high round kicks to the head is a great way to develop skill and coordination.

An advantage of the round kick is that it's easy to combine with other kicks and punches. For example, a round kick followed by a front punch is an effective combination that is easy to execute.

The student's foot position depends a lot on the target and whether or not the student is wearing shoes. If a student is not wearing shoes, he should pull the toes back and make contact with the ball or instep of the foot or with the shin. However, if the student is wearing hard-toed shoes, for example, driving the toes into an attacker's ribs can be very effective.

This kick can be used at very high speed with a lot of "snap," or it can be thrown like a club where the goal is to drive it "through" the opponent. Both methods have merit.

To teach a child how to throw a rear round kick:

Step 1. Begin by explaining the ready position, which in this case is a basic fighting stance.

Step 2. Guide the child's limbs through the motion. For the round kick, bring the rear leg forward and prepare to kick. Note that the hands are held in a ready position.

Step 3. Kick the leg out. Note how the instructor is concentrating on the child's form.

After you have "walked" them through the move a few times, have the children practice the technique on their own. Here's the round kick again without the instructor.

Step 1. The ready position.

Step 2. Bring the rear leg forward and prepare to kick.

Step 3. Kick the leg out.

Now that the basics of the move are understood, introduce a target. At this stage, the child should still be kicking without much power—proper form is the goal.

Step 1. Hold your hand out as a target. (Keep in mind that you can hold your hand a lot lower than pictured.)

Step 2. The rear leg has been brought forward in preparation.

Step 3. Instruct the student to kick your hand.

Step 4. The next stage is to begin to develop some power with the kick. A hand-held bag is ideal for this purpose.

Step 5. Instruct the student to kick the bag with some force.

A large heavy bag can be kicked at 100 percent power without damage to either partner.

FRONT KICK

The front kick is the easiest kick to learn and it's also extremely effective. The groin is the most common target, but this kick can be used to hit any part of the body. A well-placed kick to the stomach will stop most bullies; low front shin kicks are extremely effective; and a front kick/stomp to the knee can break an attacker's leg.

Raise the knee before kicking. Don't let the kids "football" the kick, which makes it easy to block. Tell them to point their knee at the target before kicking and then simply extend the leg.

Step 1. Stand in a ready position and then bring the rear leg forward and prepare to kick.

Step 2. Execute the kick and make contact with the ball of the foot. Remember to pull the toes back (you want children to injure their attackers, not themselves).

Step 1. Here's how the kick looks from the front. From the ready position, bring the rear leg forward and raise the knee.

Step 2. Kick—making contact with the ball of the foot.

Step 1. Once your student has an understanding of the kick, have her try it against a bag. The rear leg has been brought forward and has begun to kick.

Step 2. Note how the ball of the foot makes contact.

SIDE KICK

Be very careful how you instruct children to use the side kick; it has considerable bone-breaking power. A side kick to the knee can easily break a leg, and side kicks to the chest can result in broken ribs. The fact that so much damage can be done with the side kick—by almost anyone—is what makes it such an appealing and effective self-defense weapon. It is also relatively easy to develop a lot of power with the side kick early on in training.

Note that this kick is "chambered," meaning the shot is cocked (pulled back) before being executed. Not all moves are chambered because the element of surprise is imperative in many self-defense situations.

Step 1. From the ready position . . .

Step 2. . . . raise the front leg and chamber the kick.

Step 3. Kick out sideways and make contact with the heel.

Step 1. Here's how the kick looks from the front. From the ready position, lift the front leg and chamber the kick.

Step 2. Drive the kick out and make contact with the heel.

STEPPING SIDE KICK

This is the premium power kick. It's also an excellent way to close the gap between yourself and an opponent.

Step 1. Stand a few feet away from the target.

Step 2. Step the rear leg up—almost behind the front leg—and raise the front leg in preparation to kick.

Step 3. Drive the kick into the target.

Step 1. Kicking the heavy bag is an ideal way to develop power with the side kick. Step forward with the rear leg and prepare to kick. It's possible to build up a tremendous amount of momentum with the hop forward.

Step 2. Slam the kick into the bag. Remind students that they should always make contact with the heel.

SPIN KICK

This is basically a spinning side kick. The spin adds momentum which results in power. The downside is reduced speed; the spin delays impact and allows the opponent a moment to react. For this reason, I generally don't recommend using a spin kick in most self-defense situations where failure could result in deadly serious consequences. However, practicing the spin kick is a great coordination builder. It is also devastatingly powerful when thrown correctly.

Step 1. From a left-side forward ready position . . .

Step 2. . . . "spin" backwards to the right and raise the right leg in preparation.

Step 3. Drive the kick out in a straight line and make contact with the heel.

Kicks   37

Here's the spin as viewed from the side.

The kick as viewed from the side.

Step 1. Have the student practice on a bag to develop power.

Step 2. Note how the student continues to look at his target.

Step 3. Drive the heel of the foot into the bag.

Here's an example of how the spin kick can be applied.

Step 1. The defender (left) has pushed the aggressor's hand away . . .

Step 2. . . . and then continues the spin and throws a spin kick to the ribs.

FOOT STOMP

This is an excellent self-defense weapon for young children. Foot stomps to the top of the foot probably won't cause any lasting damage to a school-yard bully (whereas a side kick to the knee may permanently alter his life).

Show the child where the target is — usually the ankle or top of the foot.

Step 1. From a ready position, chamber the kick.

Step 2. Stomp down onto the target.

Step 1. To escape a shoulder grab.

Step 2. Chamber the foot stomp . . .

Step 3. . . . and stomp onto the attacker's knee, shin, ankle, or the top of the foot.

Chapter Five

HITTING WITH THE HANDS

Generally, the fastest way to strike someone is to hit them with your hands. While a hand strike may not have as much power as a kick, it's usually much faster. Why? Because a punch doesn't have to travel very far before it makes contact. A kick to the head has to cover a distance of about four to six feet (depending on the target's height) — a punch only has to travel about two feet.

Another advantage of hand strikes is they're easy to learn and remember. Some kicks can be difficult to learn, requiring several weeks of practice to master. Conversely, many hand strikes are simple enough to be learned in one lesson. Of course, the ideal situation is to teach your children how to kick *and* punch so they can choose the appropriate defense for whatever situation they may encounter. However, keep in mind that hand strikes are generally easier to learn than most kicks.

FRONT PUNCH

The front punch is a fundamental self-defense weapon. It is easy to execute, easy to remember and exceptionally effective. Anyone can learn to punch someone in the nose with a front punch, which is often all that is needed to stop a bully from further aggressive actions.

Tell your children not to telegraph that they're about to strike by chambering the punch before it's thrown. Instruct your students to throw the punch without warning — to make sure they don't pull their hand backwards before throwing the punch. There shouldn't be any indication that a punch is about to be thrown. An easy alternative to a fighting stance — which obviously telegraphs an aggressive defense — is to stand with the hands holding the lapels. This way a punch can be thrown quickly from the chest without warning the opponent by assuming a fighting stance.

Step 1. From the ready position . . .

Step 2. . . . punch straight out with the front hand.

The Parent's Guide to Teaching Self-Defense

Step 1. Note how the fist only has to travel about two feet to the bag (which represents an opponent's head).

Step 2. Don't "telegraph" the punch; it should explode straight out.

REVERSE PUNCH

The reverse punch is one of the most powerful punches in the martial arts. Its effectiveness comes from the momentum created by rotating the shoulders as the punch is thrown. Reverse (and front) punches can be easily combined with the various kicks discussed in chapter four.

Step 1. From a ready position, rotate the upper body and "corkscrew" the rear hand forward.

Step 2. Drive the punch forward.

Step 1. Here's the reverse punch as viewed from the side. Rotate the shoulders and upper body as the punch is thrown.

Step 2. Extend the punch.

The reverse punch can be thrown with a lot of power. That bag is heavy!

PALM STRIKE

The palm strike is one of the best ways to "sucker punch" a bully or mugger. The fact that it can easily be thrown from a "hands up" position contributes to its effectiveness. Playing the coward before throwing a palm strike is a good way to lower the antagonist's guard to help create an opening.

Step 1. Hold the hands up with the palms facing outward. Try to project a nonaggressive manner.

Step 2. Step back (optional) and chamber the hand.

Step 3. Drive the palm of the hand into the opponent.

Step 1. The palm strike can be thrown very fast and unexpectedly.

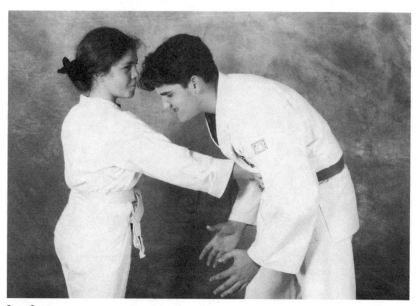

Step 2. Hit your opponent suddenly without warning.

KARATE CHOP

A chop to the throat can kill someone, so exercise caution when teaching this technique. Generally, it is not a good idea to teach young children the karate chop since it's easy to inflict serious damage with it. However, this fact also makes it an ideal self-defense weapon in life-threatening situations. A vicious inverted (palm down) chop to the throat, for example, will break the mugger's wind pipe — an excellent way to neutralize a car jacker who suddenly jumps into your daughter's vehicle.

Step 1. From a ready position . . .

Step 2. . . . chamber the front hand.

Step 3. "Chop" into the opponent's neck.

Although the neck is an ideal target, explain to your students that they can seriously hurt someone if they hit them there.

Practice target selection without actually making contact.

RIDGE HAND

It's relatively easy to knock someone out with a ridge hand. Tell your students to think of it as swinging a bat. Whip the arm through the target by leading with the shoulder. Kids usually enjoy practicing the ridge hand on a heavy bag because it's easy to generate a lot of power with this strike. The one disadvantage to a ridge hand is it's easy to block if thrown slowly.

Step 1. Start in the ready position. As the aggressor reaches for her wrist, the defender drops her left arm and prepares to throw a ridge hand.

Step 2. Swing the arm like a bat and make contact with the inside ridge of the hand. Remember to keep the thumb tucked against the palm. Note how the defender has rotated her shoulders to create power and pull her attacker off balance.

Chapter Six

BLOCKING

Learning how to block is an important skill and should not be overlooked.

The importance of being able to block an assailant's kick or punch is clear. If children can't avoid being hit, they are going to have a hard time defending themselves. Considering how important blocks are, it's ironic that many instructors don't spend sufficient time teaching and practicing blocking techniques. They train their students to hit their opponents, but fail to give them the necessary skills to avoid being hit.

I recommend you spend as much time practicing how to block kicks and punches as you do practicing how to throw offensive moves. Keep in mind that your child may not throw the first punch. If the attacker hits first, the child's ability to block will make the difference between success and failure.

Teach the kids to *always* follow up after a block with a kick or punch. This is very important. Too many people are trained to block and stop, but the assault usually doesn't stop after the first punch. Train your students to block, and then immediately follow up with a devastating blur of kicks and punches until their attacker is neutralized.

Explain the concept of "inside" line and "outside" line as it relates to a person's body. Hold your right arm out as if you had thrown a punch—then have your student block your arm to the "inside," or across your body. Next tell him to block to the "outside," which pushes your arm away from your body. Make sure students notice how much easier it is to throw a follow-up punch when they block to their outside. Also point out how an inside block closes their center line and provides a bit more protection. The idea is to get them thinking about the possibilities.

TEACHING KIDS HOW TO BLOCK
Learning how to block can be confusing for some children. Make sure you take the time to explain how the block is used. The idea is to avoid being hit or kicked. A successful block followed by a punch or kick puts your child back in charge. As you teach the blocks, encourage your students to think of situations in which each particular block would be most effective.

Step 1. Start by showing the students where they should make contact with the block. Explain how the block is used.

Step 2. "Walk" the kids through the block without any power or speed. Show them where the arm should make contact with the kick

Step 3. Once they have an understanding of the move, let them practice it against each other.

OVERHEAD BLOCK

The overhead block is a good block to use against any strike that comes from above. It is a useful block for younger children, as any attack by larger kids comes from above. Have the kids repeat the drill to your command. Once they have a basic understanding of the move, add some footwork such as a step back. Discuss ways the block might be used. If a child is being attacked by someone with a heavy club, stepping to the side as he blocks would be effective. The idea is to not be under the club as it comes down, but to deflect it to the side.

Step 1. From a ready position . . .

Step 2. . . . cross the wrists at chest level . . .

Step 3. . . . and drive the forearm upward to block.

Step 4. Cross the wrists again, but place the opposite hand on the outside.

Step 5. Drive the forearm upward to block.

The overhead block can be used against a punch.

INSIDE BLOCK

This is a very useful block that has many applications, such as pushing hands out of the way. Your child can divert the arm of an attacker who is attempting to grab him. Obviously, this is also an effective block to use against punches. As with all the blocks pictured, the inside block is demonstrated without footwork. Once the kids have an understanding of how to use the block, you can practice it from a fighting stance. Another common tactic is to step back—or forward—into a fighting stance as the block is executed.

Step 1. From a ready position, chamber the left arm as shown.

Step 2. Bring the arm down and block with the forearm.

Step 3. Return to the ready position.

Step 4. Chamber the right arm.

Step 5. Block to the inside with the right arm.

DOWNWARD BLOCK

This block is commonly used against a variety of kicks. If the child is blocking a stronger child's kick, it's important that he step to the side as he blocks. The idea is to avoid absorbing the kick's power with the block and to "ride" the kick to control it.

Step 1. From the ready position, chamber the right arm across the body as shown.

Step 2. Execute a downward block.

Step 3. After returning to a ready position, chamber the left arm across the body.

Step 4. Then execute a downward block.

DOWNWARD CROSS BLOCK

This is a strong block that can be used against a front kick. One disadvantage is that both hands are tied up during the block. However, it's often a good choice against a strong kick.

Step 1. From the ready position, raise both hands as shown. Make a fist with both hands to prevent the fingers from bending or breaking when the block is thrown.

Step 2. Slam the arms downward (crossing wrists as you go) and block. Stepping backwards on impact can help absorb the blow.

OUTSIDE BLOCK

This is another good block to use against a punch. It also "opens up" the rear hand for a follow-up punch.

Step 1. From a ready position . . .

Step 2. . . . chamber the hands as shown.

Step 3. Simultaneously bring the left arm back to the waist and swing the right arm up in a circular motion to block.

Here is the outside block using the left arm.

Step 1. Return to the ready position.

Step 2. Chamber the hands as shown.

Step 3. Simultaneously bring the right arm back to the waist and swing the left arm up in a circular outside block. A natural follow-up could be a right reverse punch.

Chapter Seven

ESCAPING CHOKES AND HOLDS

Children and women are more likely to be grabbed in a fight than are men. While men generally get into fist fights, children and women are often grabbed during the first moment of an attack. It is possible, for example, for a child to be grabbed by the wrist and dragged off the street. If your child is grabbed before she can block the incoming arm, she must be able to escape the hold before she can defend herself or get away.

Many of the wrist releases included in this chapter are based on the blocking techniques discussed in chapter six. Spend some time going over the information in chapter six before you begin to teach the maneuvers illustrated here. Your children need to be comfortable with all of the blocking motions before they can successfully execute these releases.

Choke holds and head locks are commonly encountered in the school yard. Fortunately, they're easy to get out of, and you shouldn't have any trouble teaching your students these techniques. Remind them that speed is very important—they must explode into action to be successful.

The best way to practice the following techniques is to pair the kids up and have them go through the moves slowly until they understand all the moves involved. Don't let them add any power or speed until they have the coordination worked out. You may want to don protective gear so they can try the moves out on you at full power, but don't ever let them throw kicks to the knee at full power even if you are wearing protective gear.

REAR CHOKE HOLD

Tell your children that the key to success in getting out of a choke hold is to make their move as soon as they are grabbed. It is important not to wait too long or the bully may begin to choke the strength out of them. Once you are comfortable that they have learned the basics of this move, have them practice together. To build up the needed reactions, have the kids react as soon as their partner grabs them.

Step 1. The defender has been attacked from behind and is being choked.

Step 2. Grab the assailant's arm and bend the knees to unbalance the attacker.

Step 3. Prepare to throw a chop to the groin.

Step 4. Strike the assailant in the groin.

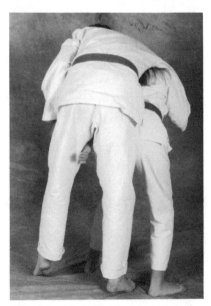

Here's the hit to the groin as viewed from the rear.

BEAR HUG

Just as in the choke hold, getting out of a bear hug requires that the victim react the moment he is grabbed. If he waits too long, the attacker may squeeze him so hard that it will be difficult to get away. Other defenses include: grabbing the groin, back kicking into the knee, and a rear head butt. If attacked from the front, the child can use a head butt, grab the groin, and kick and knee the attacker. Go over these variations with the students once they have mastered the elbow defense illustrated here.

Step 1. The defender has been grabbed from behind in a "bear hug."

Step 2. Step to the side and drop down—simultaneously throw the hands forward and prepare to elbow the attacker.

Step 3. Smash the elbow into the attacker's chest. Note how the left hand is used to add power to the blow.

Escaping Chokes and Holds   69

SINGLE WRIST GRABS

The following techniques, in addition to being useful self-defense moves, are great overall coordination builders, and children always seem to enjoy practicing them. These wrist releases are also a great way to practice the blocks discussed in chapter six.

Remember that each release must be followed up with a punch or kick. Point out to the students that their attacker will probably try to hit them if they don't strike him first. Explain that there is a certain advantage offered when someone grabs your wrist—you know where their hand is. All a wrist grab really means is that two people are attached, and either person can use that fact to his advantage. For example, tell students to use the fact that someone has grabbed them by pulling them into a front kick. This is demonstrated in the next sequence of photos.

SINGLE WRIST GRAB #1

Step 1. The defender has been grabbed by the wrist.

Step 2. Chamber the rear leg and prepare to throw a front kick.

Step 3. Front kick to the groin.

SINGLE WRIST GRAB #2

Step 1. The defender has been grabbed by the wrist.

Step 2. Prepare to throw a side kick . . .

Step 3. . . . and kick the assailant in the knee.

SINGLE WRIST GRAB #3

Step 1. The defender has been grabbed by the wrist.

Step 2. Swing the wrists upward and cross them with the free hand on the outside.

Step 3. Continue the circular motion into an overhead block and knock the attacker's hand off the wrist. Note how the right hand has been chambered to throw a punch.

SINGLE WRIST GRAB #4

Step 1. The defender has been grabbed by the wrist.

Step 2. Chamber the free hand as shown.

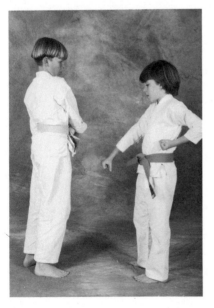

Step 3. Execute a downward block and knock the attacker's hand clear. Simultaneously chamber the left hand to throw a punch.

SINGLE WRIST GRAB #5

Step 1. The defender has been grabbed by the wrist.

Step 2. Swing the arm upward in a circular motion and simultaneously chamber the right hand.

Step 3. Rotate the shoulders and execute a block through the attacker's arm, knocking her arm clear. Note how the left hand is chambered to throw a punch.

Remember to keep training fun!

SINGLE WRIST GRAB #6

Step 1. The defender has been grabbed by the wrist.

Step 2. Swing the arm upward in a circular motion and bring the free hand across the body as shown.

Step 3. Execute an outside block to knock the attacker's hand free. Note how the left hand is chambered to throw a punch.

Step 4. Follow up with a reverse punch.

The Parent's Guide to Teaching Self-Defense

GRABBED BY BOTH WRISTS

The advantage to being grabbed by both wrists is it ties up the attacker's hands; he can't hit the child while using his hands to grab her. In addition to the following technique, keep in mind that it is also difficult for an assailant to block any kicks that are thrown when both hands are holding the child.

Step 1. The defender has been grabbed by both her wrists.

Step 2. Suddenly raise the right hand and prepare to punch downward.

Step 3. Punch down across the attacker's hand.

Step 4. Punch through the hold, breaking it. Note how the left hand is already chambered for the follow-up punch.

Step 5. Follow up with a punch to the stomach.

GRABBED BY THE HAIR

Step 1. The defender has been grabbed by the hair.

Step 2. Reach up and grab the attacker's hand.

Step 3. Twist the attacker's arm and spin to the left.

Step 4. Continue to twist the attacker's arm . . .

Step 5. . . . and bend him to the floor.

FRONT CHOKE

Speed is important here. If the child waits too long before reacting, he may begin to black out and not have the strength to fight back. Teach the kids to react as soon as they are grabbed. This cannot be stressed enough.

Step 1. The defender is being choked.

Step 2. Raise both hands up in the air.

Step 3. Rotate the upper body to the right . . .

Step 4. . . . and smash the elbows down, breaking the attacker's choke.

Step 5. Follow up with a reverse punch.

REAR CHOKE

It's important to spin around fast and aggressively in the following technique. The element of surprise should be used. To help confuse an attacker, instruct the students to yell as they go into action.

Step 1. The defender is being choked from behind.

Step 2. Throw both arms up in the air.

Step 3. Rotate to the left . . .

Step 4. . . . and push the attacker's arms to the side with the left arm while chambering the right hand for a punch.

Step 5. Hit the attacker with a reverse punch.

SHOULDER GRAB

Once again, the concept of knowing where the attacker's hand is applies here. As long as his hand is on the victim's shoulder, he can't use that hand to hit or block.

Step 1. The defender has been grabbed by the left shoulder.

Step 2. Raise the left arm into the air.

Step 3. Simultaneously "pin" the attacker's hand to the shoulder with the right hand.

Step 4. Smash the left forearm into the attacker's arm and drive him to the ground. Another option is to "pin" the hand on the shoulder and then side kick to the knee.

GRABBED ON BOTH SIDES

The key here is to use the assailants' holds as leverage when the kicks are thrown. Explain to the kids that the chance of success is high since the attackers can't easily block the kicks unless they let go of the victim. Once again, speed is very important.

Step 1. The defender has been grabbed by two people.

Step 2. Chamber the right leg for a front kick.

Step 3. Front kick the bigger assailant in the knee.

Step 4. Prepare to side kick the second assailant.

Step 5. Side kick her in the knee. Round kicks to the kidneys are also a good choice.

Chapter Eight

IN THE STREET

This chapter contains some examples of how to apply a few of the techniques discussed in the previous chapters. As with all the techniques in this book, make sure your students practice executing them with both sides of their body. For example, explain that there's no guarantee that a mugger will grab their right side, so they must be equally prepared to escape from a grab to their left.

Remember to occasionally have the kids practice in the street while wearing their everyday clothes. You don't have to do it often — once a month is enough. The idea is to help them discover any restrictions encountered by tight jeans, slippery ground, or any other obstacles that might not be present in their regular workout environment.

PICKED UP OFF THE GROUND
Small children, particularly, are in danger of being picked up and carried away.

Step 1. A stranger prepares to lift the child off the ground.

Step 2. As the stranger picks up the child, the defender throws his left arm straight up in the air . . .

Step 3. . . . and smashes his elbow into the stranger's nose.

Step 4. As soon as he's released, the child runs away.

AGAINST A WALL

This type of harassment can be encountered by children of all ages and can happen almost anywhere.

Step 1. A punk has pushed the defender against a wall.

Step 2. Push his left arm away with an outside block and simultaneously drive a palm strike under his chin.

Here's the same move as viewed from the other side.

PUSHED

Step 1. A thug is blocking the defender's path.

Step 2. Suddenly he reaches out to push her shoulder.

Step 3. Execute a left outside block . . .

Step 4. . . . and chamber the right leg for a side kick . . .

Step 5. . . . and side kick him in the stomach.

HAIR GRAB

Step 1. A punk has grabbed the defender by the hair.

Step 2. "Pin" his hand with both hands and chamber a left side kick.

Step 3. Side kick him in the knee. Don't release his hands during the kick; use the leverage to "pull" him into the kick.

Step 4. Follow up by either scraping the shin or stomping on the foot.

ATTEMPTED SHOULDER GRAB

Step 1. A thug is blocking the defender's way.

Step 2. As he reaches out to grab the left shoulder, execute a left outside block.

Step 3. Chamber the right leg for a front kick.

Step 4. Kick him in the groin.

SHOULDER GRAB

Show your kids that they can use items they may carry on a daily basis as weapons. School books, for example, can be used to strike an opponent.

Step 1. A bully is blocking the defender's path.

Step 2. Suddenly he reaches out and grabs her shoulder. Note how she is holding the books, chambered for a strike to the stomach.

Step 3. Drive the books into the bully's stomach.

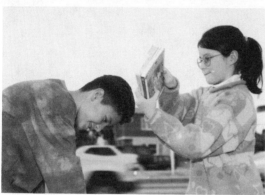

Step 4. Prepare to follow up with a strike to the head.

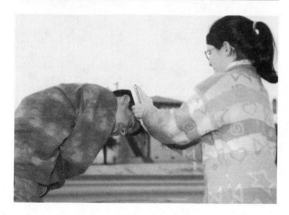

Step 5. Slam the books into the bully's head.

SLAPPED

Step 1. A punk prepares to slap the defender.

Step 2. As he swings, step back and execute a left upward block.

Step 3. The attacker prepares to strike with the other hand.

Step 4. Step back and execute a right upward block.

Step 5. Wrap the right arm around the attacker's arm, placing him in an arm lock.

Step 6. Strike him under the chin with a palm strike.

The Parent's Guide to Teaching Self-Defense

Here's the palm strike as viewed from the other side. The idea is to "snap" his head back with the blow.

Step 7. Follow him to the ground if necessary and hit him again.

PUSHED TO THE GROUND

It is important that your kids don't let an attacker get on top of them after they've been pushed to the ground, since this is a hard position to fight from. It's much easier to harm an assailant if they hit him as he approaches.

Step 1. A bully prepares to push the defender to the ground.

Step 2. After being pushed to the ground, roll to one side and prepare to kick him in the knee.

Step 3. Place one foot behind his ankle to provide leverage for the knee kick.

Step 4. Kick him in the knee with the left foot while pulling his foot forward with the right. If done with enough force, he'll be thrown to the ground.

Step 5. Always make sure your kids understand that they should run away after creating an opening.

HEAD LOCK

Step 1. A bully has grabbed the defender in a head lock and is about to punch him in the face.

Step 2. Block the punch with the left arm . . .

Step 3. . . . and grab his groin and squeeze.

Photos by Maria Doest.

PUSHED INTO A CORNER

Step 1. A thug has pushed the defender into a corner.

Step 2. Prepare to kick him in the knee.

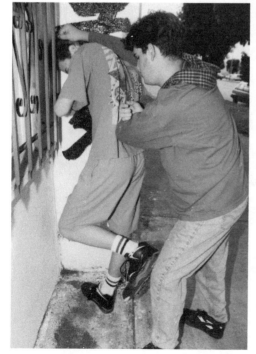

Step 3. Back kick him in the knee.

Step 4. Be prepared to strike again if necessary.

AGAINST A GANG

When there is more than one attacker, it's often sufficient to "take out" only one of them. Often the other thugs will freeze in shock during the first moment of the defense. Instruct your students always to damage the most threatening opponent (such as the biggest) first, and to run away after they've created an opening. Also point out that an older child should try to protect a younger child if they are traveling together.

Step 1. A gang of three is threatening two younger children.

Step 2. As one of the thugs reaches out to grab one of the defenders, he executes a left outside block.

Step 3. Prepare to throw a side kick . . .

Step 4. . . . and kick him in the knee and then run away.

HARASSED

Step 1. Two girls are being harassed by a couple of punks.

Step 2. Without warning, one of the girls pushes her attacker's hand away and simultaneously hits him in the chest with a reverse punch.

Step 3. Follow up with a palm strike to the chin.

Step 4. Drive his head back with the strike.

Step 5. Take advantage of the opening and run away.

FRONT GRAB

Step 1. A bully has grabbed the young defender and is demanding money.

Step 2. Raise the left hand into the air.

Step 3. Twist to the right while slamming the elbow into the attacker's arm. Note how the left hand is chambered to punch.

Step 4. Follow up with a right reverse punch to the stomach.

Step 5. Run away.

Chapter Nine

PSYCHOLOGY AND TACTICS

THINK SELF-DEFENSE

Teach your students that their brain is the most powerful weapon they possess and encourage them to think out what they would do in various scenarios. What would your daughter do if she were grabbed around the neck? What would your son do if a bully pushed him to the ground? What if they are stranded late at night and they don't have a ride home? The idea is to get the kids to think about all the possible problems they may encounter and try to work out what the solutions are.

It's surprising how quickly your students will come up with scenarios you may not have thought about. When I first started teaching children, it surprised me how many of them were concerned about being assaulted when sitting down. Apparently, many of the girls had been harassed by boys while they were sitting in the bleachers. It forced me to rethink some of the techniques I had been teaching in order to adapt them to their particular needs.

By playing the "what if" game, you can help your child discover any "holes" in information presented to her. For example, what would your child do if a pleasant-looking person holding a cute puppy offered to let her pet the animal?

While most parents tell children the standard lines about not talking to strangers and not accepting candy or food from strangers, keep in mind that criminals are becoming more devious. Abductors now use a frighteningly convincing array of ploys to draw children in. Imagine yourself in the role of a kidnapper. How would you behave? By preparing for all types of possible scenarios, you can help cut down on the odds of your child becoming a victim.

FIRST STRIKE

Many of the concepts discussed in this chapter must be adapted to your child's particular situation. The idea of hitting first, making the first strike, is a good example. In a true self-defense situation—such as your daughter defending herself against a would-be rapist—hitting first is critical. Conversely, if you are dealing with a seven-year-old child, encouraging him to swing at the first sign of trouble could lead to disastrous results.

In a life-threatening defense situation, it's critical for children to launch their attack before their assailant's. Many people have the misconception that they should let the other party "swing first." This can be a deadly mistake. For example, if a two-hundred-pound rapist has the opportunity to strike your daughter first, she may not recover. Her only choices are either to submit completely (to avoid being killed) or to launch a devastating attack against her assailant that leaves him crippled and incapable of further aggressions. If a child isn't prepared to hit first and continue her onslaught until the attacker is disabled, she shouldn't attempt to defend herself. A halfhearted attack that fails will probably only aggravate the situation.

Once again, I'd like to point out that the concept of hitting first generally shouldn't be carried into the school yard. Impress upon your students that they should only use their ability to defend themselves, not pick fights.

SCREAMING

Combining self-defense with a loud yell has two advantages. First, it psyches the child up as she launches her attack. Second, it may momentarily "freeze" her opponent into nonreaction. A good way to demonstrate this to your class is to suddenly stop in front of one of your students while you are talking and yell "hey" as loud as you can. They will probably all freeze in shock. Explain that their attacker can also be stunned by a loud yell at the same instant they begin their defense.

The traditional karate yell is "ki-ah" (pronounced kee-ah) and is said in one exhalation. Have the class practice yelling as they kick and punch.

Noise is a form of self-defense in itself. Sometimes all that may be needed to deter an attack is a loud scream. A pervert attempting to abduct a child may give up the attempt if the child's screams are loud enough to draw attention. Keep in mind, however, that a young child screaming in the presence of an adult may not draw attention from onlookers who may think it's simply an annoyed or upset child responding to the parent.

Instruct the kids to scream and repeat "kidnapper" as loud as they can or "you're hurting me." It's a difficult situation because it's actually hard to draw people's attention since screaming kids are fairly common. Whatever you do, discourage a simple scream because it will surely be ignored.

There's a danger in making noise, too. An attacker may panic and decide to injure the child to prevent people from hearing him. Since you know your particular environment and child better than I do, you must decide what advice is best. One consideration is the child's age. Young children's only defense may be to scream and make noise. If they are about to be abducted, it's better that they attempt to get some attention from a bystander regardless of the risk. A teenager, however, may have the physical size and strength to physically fend off an adult. In that situation, silence before launching a defense may be a better choice.

In the school yard, where children are likely to be defending themselves against other children, encourage them to yell as they launch their attack to momentarily stun their opponent.

CHOICES

Explain to your students that they have three options if they are assaulted.

Run Away

They can run away and avoid the confrontation altogether. There's nothing wrong with this option; in fact, it's often the best choice. Don't encourage kids to stand their ground at all costs.

Give In

Children can give in to attackers — even rapists. I understand this is a horrible thought, but let's be honest. If your children don't have the skill necessary to defend themselves in certain situations, encouraging them to fight may cost them their lives. For example, if a rapist holds a gun to a young girl's head, do you really want her to fight back? The answer might be yes, but it's a judgment call. The point is that submitting to the attacker is better than dying.

On a less serious level, handing over a bag of candy to three school-yard bullies might be a better solution than engaging in a fight, especially if your child is half the weight and size of any of the antagonists. Make sure that you don't give your child the impression that he must physically defend himself at any cost.

Defend Themselves

Physical self-defense is obviously an option. I always tell students not to attempt self-defense unless they are prepared to see it through. This applies to the school yard as well as the street. It's simple, really. The chances of becoming injured are much greater in a fight than if they simply walk away.

AVOIDING TROUBLE

One of the best defenses is to avoid unpleasant encounters if possible. Explain the following concepts to your children so they can reduce the risk of being caught alone.

Travel in a Group

A child walking alone is a much more inviting target than a group of children. Encourage your child to always go out with friends, brothers and sisters, or adults. Obviously, young children should never be allowed to wander unattended.

Abductions can happen anywhere. A friend of mine recently left his child playing in front of their house while he carried some groceries inside. When he returned to the front of the house, he saw a car that had slowed down and opened the passenger door—and two men inside the car were talking to his five-year-old daughter. When they saw the adult come out of the house, they closed the door and rapidly drove away. It would appear that an abduction might have taken place if the child had been left alone a few moments longer. The lesson is clear.

Be Aware

Children can get very caught up in what they are doing and may completely ignore their surroundings. Explain that they should always be on the lookout for suspicious strangers. For example, if your child spots someone observing him from a parked car, he should immediately seek responsible adults and notify them of the situation.

It's equally important for your children to understand that certain environments are more dangerous than others. A back alley is not an ideal playground. Walking through parks late at night can also be a risky activity and should be discouraged. The point is to educate your children so they will be aware of their environment and the people in it.

MISDIRECTION

Misdirection or feinting is an important tactic in self-defense. An example of a feint would be raising one hand in the air to make the other person look up — and then kicking the opponent in the lower body. It's often said that if two opponents of equal skill and size get into a fight, the one who has mastered the art of using misdirection will win.

Explain the concept of misdirection to your students after they have become proficient with the basic kicks and punches. Misdirection can be applied in many ways. Pretending to hit "high" a moment before striking "low" is a simple example. You will probably come up with some other types of feints.

It's equally important to show kids how they can create misdirection before launching a self-defense technique. Show them that they can use things they are carrying to create distraction. For example, a purse thrown toward a rapist's head may distract him for a moment while your daughter lands a vicious kick to the groin. Schoolbooks, backpacks, portable cassette players and hats can all be used to distract an attacker and create an opening.

I teach students very early on how to use these tactics. The idea is to help ensure the element of surprise when they make their move. You can introduce this concept once the class knows a few kicks and punches.

Show the kids other ways to create distractions that will help them in difficult situations. What would they do if they were thrown to the ground and the attacker was about to continue his aggression? A handful of dirt or sand thrown violently into the mugger's face might blind him long enough for the victim to injure the troublemaker and get away.

GENDER DIFFERENCES

Girls and boys often grow up with different views about violent behavior. For example, boys grow up wrestling in the school yard, fighting with siblings, and are generally raised to believe that it is socially acceptable to fend off an aggressor with violence. Conversely, girls are generally raised to believe that it is unladylike to resort to physical violence. As a self-defense instructor, part of your job is to help female students overcome any inhibitions they may have about violence. Obviously, there are girls who have no such qualms, just as there are boys who will need this extra encouragement to overcome their inhibitions.

Actually, there are some definite advantages to being female in a self-defense situation. One of the reasons some thieves pick on women is they don't expect them to fight back, which definitely gives a girl the advantage. Explain to your daughter that she shouldn't give up the element of surprise by advertising the fact that she is prepared to defend herself. Dropping into a karate stance and yelling, ''Come and get it, scumbag,'' will only alert her attackers that they are in for a fight.

It is much more effective for a girl to cower in fear and shy away before unleashing a devastating attack upon her assailants. This philosophy can also be applied by any young person. Most people don't expect a physical retaliation from a young child, male or female. Naturally, I'm not suggesting that this tactic would enable young children to overpower an adult, but it may give them a tactical advantage in some situations.

On the other hand, there may be situations when an aggressive show of force may be all that is needed to stop an attack. It is a judgment call, but if your child truly believes that she must physically defend herself, it's better to play possum before fighting.

Wearing protective armor yourself so your daughter can attack you at 100 percent power is a terrific way to develop her ability. Some girls have never hit anyone and may have trouble adapting to the concept. Encourage them to hit as hard as they can once they've learned the basics. Sparring with you and other adults (particularly males) is an excellent way to help them get over inhibitions. It's important to help timid children become comfortable with the concept of hitting another person if they have to defend themselves.

Chapter Ten

STYLES AND SCHOOLS

After you've spent some time teaching your children basic self-defense with the information presented in this book, you may decide to continue their martial arts education by enrolling them in a formal class. This is a good idea since martial arts classes offer a lot of benefits. While you may be able to teach your youngsters the basics of self-defense, an organized school can take them much further. For example, wouldn't you like to see your child earn a black belt? Another advantage to large classes is they provide your child with the opportunity to practice against kids of different sizes, which can build skill and confidence.

STYLES

One of the first decisions you'll have to make when picking a martial arts school is the style you want your child to study. There are a bewildering number of styles from which to choose. Some schools focus on kicks, while others favor hand techniques; a few rely primarily on throws, and some instructors primarily teach chokes and holds.

So what's best? Well, it's a personal decision that your child should be involved in. One style is not better than another, but individuals will excel within a martial art that lends itself to their particular strengths and weaknesses. For example, if your child likes to kick a lot, tae kwon do may be for him. If she prefers hand techniques, then wing chun class may be more fun. Put a child who likes to box in a tae kwon do class, and he'll probably become bored.

Here's a breakdown of some of the more popular styles you may encounter.

Aikido

Aikido features locks, throws, and grappling techniques — it's a lot of fun to learn. This style teaches students how to use an opponent's momentum to their advantage, and it is an excellent style for children who may be faced with an attacker who is much bigger and stronger. The disadvantage of aikido is that it's fairly specialized and doesn't give children a wide overview of the martial arts. You may want to wait to enroll children in an aikido class until they've spent a few years in a basic karate class.

Boxing

Boxing is an excellent form of self-defense. A big advantage of boxing is that students get a lot of sparring time, which translates into becoming comfortable with the timing involved in a fight. Boxers also get used to being hit—which is important.

The disadvantage of boxing is the fact that students get hit a lot in sparring. Young people shouldn't be exposed to a lot of head contact, and some children may find the sport too physical. Boxing also doesn't provide children with much variety in its techniques. Learning to kick and punch and how to get out of various chokes and holds is fun for most children. However, boxing will teach your kids how to fight.

Judo

Judo features a lot of throwing and choking techniques. While judo is a good form of self-defense, it's primarily thought of as a sport. Judo is an Olympic sport.

Like aikido, judo teaches practitioners how to overcome a larger opponent by using the attacker's weight and momentum against him. During a match, students hold each other by the gi and attempt to execute a throw. It's a lot of fun to learn and practice.

Judo has the added advantage of teaching kids how to take a fall. Overall, judo is a good choice for children who don't like kicking and punching.

Kempo Karate

Kempo is an all-around style that puts equal emphasis on kicks and hand techniques. Kempo is an excellent martial art to start children in because it teaches very solid basics. Kicks are fairly simple and effective, and the hand techniques put a lot of emphasis on power. In fact, "power" is probably the best word to describe kempo.

Shorin-ryu Karate

This Okinawan style is another excellent martial art for children. As with kempo, students come away with a strong understanding of the basics, which can be applied regardless of what styles they choose to study later in life. Shorin-ryu gives equal emphasis to kicks and punches and features very practical techniques. There isn't a lot of "flash" in this style.

Shotokan

This is another solid, traditional style that emphasizes basics. Strong stances, fairly simple kicks and punches, and various sweeps and take-downs are taught to students early on. Like kempo and shorin-ryu, shotokan is a good all-around style for most children.

Tae Kwon Do

This Korean martial art is known for its wild, aerial kicks. Children who like to kick will most likely enjoy tae kwon do. It's an effective form of self-defense that also has a high profile as a sport. Tae kwon do recently became an Olympic event.

Tae kwon do is very organized as a style. For example, a brown belt in California will have been taught the same techniques as a brown belt in Vermont. While this is the goal of all the styles with a ranking system, it's not always the case. I've been to places where the techniques taught were so different between schools that a person's rank couldn't be honored. This generally won't happen with tae kwon do.

Wing Chun Kung Fu

Wing chun primarily features hand techniques along with a few kicks. It's an excellent style for fighting up close, but generally isn't a good first style for most children since kicks are somewhat neglected in wing chun. However, wing chun does teach practitioners how *not* to get hit and how to fight in close.

One reason I don't recommend wing chun for young children is the training involves a lot of punching padded walls and wooden dummies, which could damage young bones. Older teenagers, however, may thrive in a wing chun class.

Wushu Kung Fu

Wushu is the official Chinese word for kung fu. While not a practical martial art, wushu is one of the most spectacular styles to watch. Amazing feats of aerial limberness are incorporated into some of the style's forms. Your child will certainly benefit from the training wushu offers; the limberness, strength, and coordination developed can be applied in any form of self-defense.

Soft Styles vs. Hard Styles

You may hear people referring to a particular style as being "hard" or "soft." Basically, a hard style, such as kempo karate, relies on strength more than a soft style. Blocking a punch with an inside block—without moving out of the way—is a hard-style technique. Redirecting an opponent's punch while stepping to the side is a soft-style technique.

Generally, hard styles are preferred by strong, physical people, while soft styles are often preferred by people who expect to encounter opponents of greater strength. There's also a lot of crossover between hard and soft techniques within some of the systems. The point is, most martial arts can generally be defined as either hard or soft styles and you want to consider such a definition when choosing styles.

SCHOOLS

Once you've settled on a style for your child, you'll have to choose a school. Depending on where you live and what style you've chosen, there may be two or three different schools near your home that teach the same style. In Los Angeles, for example, there are about six tae kwon do schools, and they're by no means equal in terms of equipment, cost, and quality of instruction. Before you put down your hard-earned money to pay for your child's self-defense classes, there are many things to consider.

Cost

How much do the classes cost? There's a wide range of possibilities in this area. Some schools charge a monthly fee of about $50, and the children's classes meet about three times a week. Other schools want you to sign a contract that commits you to several months of payment, regardless of whether or not your child stays with the class for the duration of the agreement.

Generally, it's best to avoid the contracts. I say "generally" because in some instances it may be unavoidable. For example, the best tae kwon do school in my area won't accept students unless they sign a contract committing them to about $600 in payments, but they also provide a full gym, unlimited classes, and a world-famous instructor. Conversely, there's a wing chun school a few miles from my home that offers classes for $60 a month, and it is also taught by a world-famous instructor. If you want your child to learn tae kwon do from the best in Los Angeles, you won't have a choice and will have to sign the contract.

However, you must also look at your purposes. Do beginning students really need a world-class instructor? Probably not. Shop around before shelling out your dollars; there are a lot of options available.

Belts and Ranks

Does the school award belts and ranks? Generally, karate, judo, and tae kwon do schools have a ranking system while kung fu schools don't. If a kung fu school does have a ranking system, it often differentiates only between the novices and the experts.

The traditional system of earning colored belts has some advantages for children. Meeting specific goals, such as earning a yellow belt, can provide children with a sense of accomplishment. It also gives them a tangible measure of their progress. A long-range goal, such as earning black belt, can keep children motivated in a self-defense class.

Credentials

Check the teacher's credentials. A qualified martial arts instructor will have, at the very least, a certificate of rank from a reputable organization. A few phone calls to some of the martial arts magazines will help you to determine if the instructor's certifying organization is legitimate.

There are some excellent instructors out there who are affiliated with organizations that may not be nationally known. If this seems to be the case, talk with some of the students (and parents) and see if they're satisfied with the quality of the instruction.

One of the best ways to judge a school is to watch a class. In fact, I'd avoid any school that won't let you and your child watch one of its classes before enrolling. After you've visited a few schools, you'll be able to tell which ones are offering quality instruction and which ones are teaching "fluff."

Equipment

How much equipment does the school have? At the very least, the school should have a heavy bag, numerous hand-held bags, protective sparring equipment, and a large mirror. While it's not critical that a school have a lot of equipment, it certainly is helpful.

How much equipment a school has is often related to how much they charge. For example, the tae kwon do school mentioned previously has a full gym with weights and various other types of conditioning equipment. There is also a locker room with a couple of showers. It is possible to work out so completely at this facility that a health club membership isn't needed. However, is that really what your child needs? If not, why pay a high tuition for a lot of sports equipment that your kids will never use? Conversely, you probably want to avoid schools that look as though they're operating on a shoestring budget and can't afford protective sparring equipment.

CONCLUSION

Remember, whatever style and school you choose, or if you decide to do minimal training at home, have fun! You *do* want to impress upon your children that there are dangers out there and you want to prepare them to deal with them — but, most important, you want them to be able to be children. This means enjoying the training. If they begin to dread practice, talk to them and find out why. This should be a pleasant learning experience for you and your children.

INDEX

A

Age, starting, 3-4
Attempted shoulder grab, 98-99
Avoiding trouble, 120-121
Awareness, 120-121

B

Basic fighting stance, 20-22
Bear hugs, 69
Belts, 127
Blocking, 53-65
  downward block, 61-62
  downward cross block, 63
  importance, 53
  inside block, 59-60
  inside line, 54
  outside block, 64-65
  outside line, 54
  overhead block, 56-58
  slaps, 102-105
  teaching, 54
Both sides, grabbed on, 89-90
Boxing, 124

C

Chokes, 66-90
  bear hugs, 69
  front choke, 83-84
  rear choke, 85-86
  rear choke hold, 67-68
Chop, karate, 50-51
Clothing, 5
Corner, pushed into, 109-110
Cost of schools, 126-127
Credentials, schools, 127-128

D

Double wrist grab, 79-80
Downward block, 61-62

Downward cross block, 63

E

Emotional sensitivity, 9-10
Equipment
  practice sessions, 16-18
  schools, 128

F

Feinting, 121
First strike, 117-118
Foot stomp, 41-42
Front choke, 83-84
Front grab, 115-116
Front kick, 30-32
Front punch, 43-45
Full-contact sparring, 16

G

Gangs, 111-112
Gender differences, 122
Giving in, 119-120
Ground
  picked up off, 91-92
  pushed to, 106-107
Groups, traveling in, 120

H

Hair, grabbed by, 81-82, 96-97
Hands, hitting with—see Hitting.
Harassment, 113-114
Hard styles, 126
Head lock, 108
Hitting, 43-52
  front punch, 43-45
  karate chop, 50-51
  palm strike, 48-49
  reverse punch, 46-47
  ridge hand, 52

Holds, 66-90
  attempted shoulder grab, 98-99
  bear hugs, 69
  both sides, grabbed on, 89-90
  double wrist grab, 79-80
  front choke, 83-84
  front grab, 115-116
  hair, grabbed by, 81-82, 96-97
  head lock, 108
  rear choke, 67-68, 85-86
  shoulder grab, 87-88, 100-101
    attempted, 98-99
  single wrist grabs, 69-78
    number five, 75-76
    number four, 74
    number one, 70-71
    number six, 77-78
    number three, 73
    number two, 72

I
Inside block, 59-60
Inside line, 54
Introduction, 1-5

J
Judo, 124

K
Karate
  kempo karate, 124
  shorin-ryu karate, 125
Karate chop, 50-51
Katas, 18
Kempo karate, 124
Kicks, 23-42
  foot stomp, 41-42
  front kick, 30-32
  round kick, 25-29
  sequence of instruction, 23
  side kick, 33-34
  spin kick, 37-40
  stepping side kick, 35-36
  warming up, 24
Kung fu
  wing chun kung fu, 125
  wushu kung fu, 126

L
Light-contact free sparring, 15-16

M
Misdirection, 121

N
No-contact free sparring, 14-15

O
One-step contact, 14
One-step sparring, 13-14
Outside block, 64-65
Outside line, 54
Overhead block, 56-58

P
Palm strike, 48-49
Philosophy, 6-9
Picked up off ground, 91-92
Practice sessions, 12-19
  equipment, 16-18
  frequency, 18-19
  full-contact sparring, 16
  katas, 18
  length, 19
  light-contact free sparring, 15-16
  no-contact free sparring, 14-15
  one-step contact, 14
  one-step sparring, 13-14
  sparring, 12-16
Psychology, 117-122
  avoiding trouble, 120-121
  awareness, 120-121

feinting, 121
first strike, 117-118
gender differences, 122
giving in, 119-120
misdirection, 121
running away, 119
screaming, 118-119
self-defense, 120
thinking self-defense, 117
traveling in groups, 120
Punches
front punch, 43-45
reverse punch, 46-47
Pushed, 94-95
into corner, 109-110
to ground, 106-107

Q

Qualifications, teaching, 1

R

Ranks, 127
Realistic views, 4-5
Rear choke, 67-68, 85-86
Responsibility, teaching, 10-11
Reverse punch, 46-47
Ridge hand, 52
Round kick, 25-29
Running away, 119

S

Schools, 126-128
belts, 127
cost, 126-127
credentials, 127-128
equipment, 128
ranks, 127
teacher credentials, 127-128
Screaming, 118-119
Self defense
defined, 1

sport defense versus, 2-3
Sequence of instruction, 23
Shorin-ryu karate, 125
Shotokan, 125
Shoulder grab, 87-88, 100-101
attempted, 98-99
Side kick, 33-34
stepping side kick, 35-36
Simplicity, teaching, 6
Single wrist grabs, 69-78
number five, 75-76
number four, 74
number one, 70-71
number six, 77-78
number three, 73
number two, 72
Slaps, 102-105
Soft styles, 126
Sparring, 12-16
full-contact sparring, 16
light-contact free sparring, 15-16
no-contact free sparring, 14-15
one-step contact, 14
one-step sparring, 13-14
Spin kick, 37-40
Sport defense
self defense versus, 2-3
Stances
basic fighting stance, 20-22
Starting age, 3-4
Stepping side kick, 35-36
Stomp, foot, 41-42
Street defense, 91-116
front grab, 115-116
gangs, 111-112
hair, grabbed by, 96-97
harassment, 113-114
head lock, 108
picked up off ground, 91-92
pushed, 94-95
pushed into corner, 109-110

pushed to ground, 106-107
shoulder grab, 100-101
   attempted, 98-99
slaps, 102-105
wall, against, 93
Strike, palm, 48-49
Styles, 123-126
aikido, 123-124
boxing, 124
hard, 126
judo, 124
kempo karate, 124
shorin-ryu karate, 125
shotokan, 125
soft, 126
tae kwon do, 125
wing chun kung fu, 125
wushu kung fu, 126

T

Tactics, 117-122
avoiding trouble, 120-121
awareness, 120-121
feinting, 121
first strike, 117-118

gender differences, 122
giving in, 119-120
misdirection, 121
running away, 119
screaming, 118-119
self-defense, 120
traveling in groups, 120
Tae kwon do, 125
Teacher credentials, 127-128
Thinking self-defense, 117
Traveling in groups, 120

W

Wall, against, 93
Warming up, 24
Wing chun kung fu, 125
Wrist releases, 66-90
single wrist grabs, 69-78
   number five, 75-76
   number four, 74
   number one, 70-71
   number six, 77-78
   number three, 73
   number two, 72
Wushu kung fu, 126

More Books in The Parent's Guide *Series*

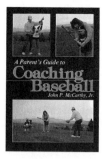  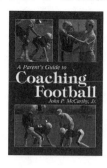 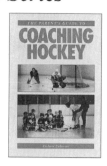

Your influence as a coach or teacher can give children (both yours and others) the greatest gifts of all: strong self-confidence and high self-esteem. *The Parent's Guide* series has nearly a dozen books full of helpful illustrations and step-by-step instructions on how to nurture and encourage children as they strive for success in sports and the arts. Plus, the friendly, familiar tone of each book will help both you and the child have fun as you learn.

The Parent's Guide to Coaching Baseball *#70076/128 pages/$7.95, paperback*

The Parent's Guide to Coaching Basketball *#70077/136 pages/$7.95, paperback*

The Parent's Guide to Coaching Football *#70078/144 pages/$7.95, paperback*

The Parent's Guide to Coaching Hockey *#70216/176 pages/$8.95, paperback*

The Parent's Guide to Coaching Soccer *#70079/136 pages/$8.95, paperback*

The Parent's Guide to Coaching Tennis *#70080/144 pages/$7.95, paperback*

The Parent's Guide to Coaching Skiing *#70217/144 pages/$8.95, paperback*

The Parent's Guide to Teaching Music *#70082/136 pages/$7.95, paperback*

The Parent's Guide to Band and Orchestra *#70075/136 pages/$7.95, paperback*

The Parent's Guide to Teaching Art: How to Encourage Your Child's Artistic Talent and Ability *#70081/184 pages/$11.95, paperback*

Use the order form below (photocopy acceptable) and save when you order two or more books!

- -

☐ **Yes!** I want the following books to help my child grow:

Book #	Brief title	Price
_____	_____	_____
_____	_____	_____
_____	_____	_____

Visa/MasterCard Orders Call TOLL-FREE
1-800-289-0963

*Add $3 postage and handling for one book; postage is FREE when you order 2 or more books.

Subtotal _____

Tax (Ohio residents only, 5.5%) _____

Postage & handling* _____

Total _____

Check enclosed $ _____   ☐ Visa   ☐ MasterCard

Acct # _____ Exp. _____

Name _____ Signature _____

Address _____

City _____ State _____ Zip _____

Stock may be limited on some titles; prices subject to change without notice.
Mail to: Betterway Books, 1507 Dana Ave., Cincinnati, OH 45207

Write to this address for a catalog of Betterway Books, plus information on *Writer's Digest* magazine, *Story* magazine, Writer's Digest Book Club, Writer's Digest School, and Writer's Digest Criticism Service.   3131